IT'S TRUE!

EVEREST
KILLS

Did you know that frogs are cannibals,
fashion can be fatal and the dinosaurs
never died? Or that redheads were
once burned at the stake as witches?
Find out why rubbish tips are like lasagna,
and how maggots help solve crimes!

Books to make
your brain bulge!
Find out all about them on
www.itstrue.com.au

KIM WILSON
PICTURES BY ANDREW PLANT

IT'S TRUE!

EVEREST
KILLS

ALLEN&UNWIN

For Finn.

May your life be full of adventures.

First published in 2006

Allen & Unwin
83 Alexander Street
Crows Nest NSW 2065
Australia
Phone: (61 2) 8425 0100
Fax: (61 2) 9906 2218
Email: info@allenandunwin.com
Web: www.allenandunwin.com

National Library of Australia
Cataloguing-in-Publication entry:

Wilson, Kim, 1969– .
It's true! Everest kills.
Bibliography.
Includes index.
For children.
ISBN 1 74114 414 0.
1. Mountaineering – Everest, Mount (China/Tibet and Nepal) – Juvenile
literature. 2. Mountaineers – Everest, Mount (China/Tibet and Nepal) –
Juvenile literature. 3. Everest, Mount (China/Tibet and Nepal) – Juvenile
literature. I. Plant, Andrew.
II. Title. (Series : It's true ; 22)
796.522095496

Series, cover and text design by Ruth Grüner
Cover photographs: Getty Images/Michael Gallacher
and Andrew Plant (background)
Set in 12.5pt Minion by Ruth Grüner
Printed by McPherson's Printing Group

1 3 5 7 9 10 8 6 4 2

**Teaching notes for the It's True! series are available
on the website: www.itstrue.com.au**

CONTENTS

WHY EVEREST?

Because it's there! Well, that's what famous mountaineer George Mallory once said when a cheeky journalist asked him the same question. But there are lots of great reasons to write about the world's highest mountain. Did you know that Mount Everest is so close to space, the sky is black? Or that at Base Camp, you sleep on a river of ice (which creaks and moans beneath you)? Or that mountains can make you crazy enough to walk off a cliff, see people who aren't there or strip naked in sub-zero temperatures? It's true!

There's awesome facts, spooky mysteries and best of all, death-defying stories of brave adventurers. My own mountain experience is rather less inspiring: on finally stumbling up a snowy 6000-metre pass in Nepal, I groaned and threw up green bile in front of a friend's camera! Apart from a sore stomach and a less-than-glamorous photo, it gave me a deep admiration for mountaineers – their bravery, their determination, and their cast-iron stomachs . . . And not just the record-holders like Edmund Hillary and Tenzing Norgay, but the many people who find their own challenges to face, their own mountains to climb. I hope you find yours.

Take care, and happy adventuring!

Kim

1

THE BIG ONE

If you've ever scrambled up a tall tree, or walked to the top of a big hill, you'll know the thrill of climbing higher and higher. So imagine how incredible it must feel to climb the highest mountain in the world – Mount Everest!

HOW HIGH IS MOUNT EVEREST EXACTLY?

Well, that's a tricky question. For a long time it was thought to be 8848 metres high, but in 2000 the latest high-tech gizmos showed it to be 8850 metres high. That's about as high as an aeroplane flies.

But even that isn't the *exact* height of Mount Everest because it's growing all the time. Yes, it grows by about six millimetres a year! And that's not all – the Himalayan mountain range in which Everest sits is moving north-east at a rate of one millimetre a week.

How is this possible? Place two pieces of paper flat on your kitchen bench. With a hand on each, push them so they crash into each other. Did one or both pieces of paper crumple and pop up as they collided? That's what is happening in the Himalaya right now: two plates of the Earth's crust are slowly smashing into each other and pushing up mountains. Mount Everest is only 50 million years old (that's young for a mountain!) so it is still growing and moving.

Scientists think the same thing happened in Australia millions of years ago, but because Australia is very old in geological terms,

WILL YOU HURRY UP! IT'S GETTING TALLER ALL THE TIME!!

its mountains have worn down over time. Australia's highest peak, Mount Kosciuszko, is only 2228 metres!

WHERE IN THE WORLD IS THE HIMALAYA?

Although Mount Everest is moving, one millimetre a week isn't very fast, so it's easy to find if you go to the right place. And the right place is Nepal – a little mountain kingdom sandwiched between Tibet* and India. Today Nepal welcomes many tourists and mountain climbers, but 150 years ago the king wouldn't

* Much of historic Tibet has now been absorbed by the People's Republic of China, with a small area known as the Tibet Autonomous Region retaining some measure of independence, though the area is still the subject of much dispute. We have referred to this area simply as 'Tibet'.

let foreigners into his country. Explorers could only gaze at the beautiful mountains from over the border in India. Some brave adventurers did sneak in by disguising themselves in local costumes and smearing their faces with boot polish!

PEAK XV

Back in the 1850s, everyone believed Kanchenjunga was the highest mountain in the Himalayan range. But then Radhanath Sikhdar, a number-cruncher in the British army in India, used instruments and tricky calculations to work out that peak XV (fifteen) was 8839.8 metres high. This made it the highest mountain in the world. He must have been very good at maths because laser measurements now show he was almost exactly right.

The Surveyor General didn't want such a grand mountain to be called 'peak XV' any more, so he named it after his old boss, Sir George Everest. (Perhaps he wanted a pay rise!) Sir George protested that his surname couldn't be translated into the local Hindi language, but the name stuck.

WHAT'S IN A NAME?

Long before Mount Everest was called peak XV, the people of Nepal knew it as Sagarmatha, which means 'Goddess of the Sky'. Tibetans call it Chomolungma, which means 'Goddess Mother of the World'. They think of it as a goddess because the snow from this mountain (and its Himalayan brothers and sisters) supplies water to millions of people, and it is big and beautiful and able to kill if people are not respectful when climbing.

Himalaya is made up of two words – *hima* meaning snow and *alaya* meaning home. So Himalaya means 'home of the snows' – which makes sense as there's snow on these mountains all year round, even in summer.

MAD MAURICE AND THE MOUNTAIN

As soon as the world's highest mountain was found, people wanted to climb it. One of the first – and the craziest! – was Maurice Wilson. Maurice was born in

1898 in England and fought in the trenches of World War I when he was 18 years old. After being shot in the chest and arm, and getting a medal for his trouble, he decided he could do anything if he had faith and determination.

In 1934, he planned to prove it by flying to Mount Everest, landing his Gypsy Moth plane on the mountain and then climbing to the summit. It didn't worry him that: (a) in the 1930s most planes didn't have enough power to fly as high as Mount Everest; (b) the Nepalese government wouldn't let him into the country; (c) many fit, experienced climbers had failed to reach the summit and he'd never climbed anything higher than a small hill; and (d) he had no idea how to fly a plane.

He trained by regularly walking to visit his parents (who lived 420 kilometres away!) and going on hill-hiking holidays. He also took a few flying lessons. When he crashed his plane, he received a letter from the British Air Ministry saying he wasn't allowed to fly anywhere (let alone to Nepal). He tore up the letter and took off anyway. The British government made sure he was denied fuel at some stopovers and he had to fly around whole countries because he wasn't allowed in their airspace. Amazingly, he and his little plane (which he named *Ever-wrest*) made it

IF I COULD JUST FIND SOMEWHERE TO LAND...

to India in one piece ... where the British authorities took *Ever-wrest* away. Still determined to get to the summit, Maurice hired three of the local Sherpa people to help him and walked into Tibet disguised as a monk. (Sherpas, who've lived in this area for generations, are famous for their strength in the mountains and many are employed as climbing guides for expeditions.) Along the way, he practised deep breathing and going without food, as he believed this would help him get to the summit.

DIARY OF MAURICE WILSON

WED - Final preparations.
THURS - Off to Everest at last!
THURS - After a week's flying, found myself back at home. Will take map this time.

FRI - Home again. Map of England insufficient. Will buy India map.
SAT - Lost my way to map shop. Must take street directory.
SUN - Found map shop. Found it was closed. Will have tea as soon as I have found cup.

On 16 April 1934, weighed down by a 20-kilogram pack, he left the Sherpas and set off up the mountain. He still knew nothing about Himalayan climbing and its dangers. Even when he was lucky enough to find a pair of abandoned crampons (metal frames that clip onto your boots to help you walk in ice and snow – see page 49 for more), he didn't have the good sense to put them on his feet! His first attempt lasted nine days, and he returned to the Sherpas exhausted, freezing and sick. He hadn't even made it to the top of the glacier! The second time, he took two Sherpas with him but a storm set in. The Sherpas begged him not to go on, but he set off alone again, waving cheerfully, carrying his tent, some bread and oatmeal, a camera and a silk Union Jack signed by some girlfriends. On 31 May 1934 he wrote the last entry in his diary: 'Off again, gorgeous day.'

REAPPEARING REMAINS

No one was particularly surprised when Maurice Wilson didn't come back. A year later, some climbers found boots, a flag, a diary and the remains of a tent scattered at North Col (7041 metres). Then they found the body of Maurice Wilson. He'd died of exhaustion and exposure in his tent. They wrapped him in what was left of the tent, lowered his body into a crevasse (a big crack in the ice), built a memorial of stones and read aloud the story of his life from his diary.

But that wasn't the last anyone saw of Maurice Wilson. From time to time, parts of his body have come to the surface as the glacier has moved: a piece of clothing, or a bit of his arm (ugh!). The most recent sighting was in 1999 when a leg bone and part of his back was found. As one climber said, 'Even in death, he shows his determination by refusing to be buried.'

MONSTER MOUNTAINS!

There are 14 mountains in the world that are higher than 8000 metres, and most are in the Himalaya.

But guess what? Even they're not the biggest mountains we know of. On Mars there's a volcano called Olympus Mons that's 27 000 metres high. (That's 27 kilometres high, or three times as high as Mount Everest!)

HIGHS AND LOWS

The summit of Mount Everest is the highest place on Earth above sea level. But the tallest mountain from base to summit is actually Mauna Kea in Hawaii, which measures 10 204 metres from its base on the sea floor to its summit. It doesn't look very big because most of it is under the sea.

Challenger Deep, in the Pacific Ocean, is the lowest place on Earth. It is part of the Marianas Trench and goes down 10 119.5 metres from sea level, so it's deeper than Mount Everest is high.

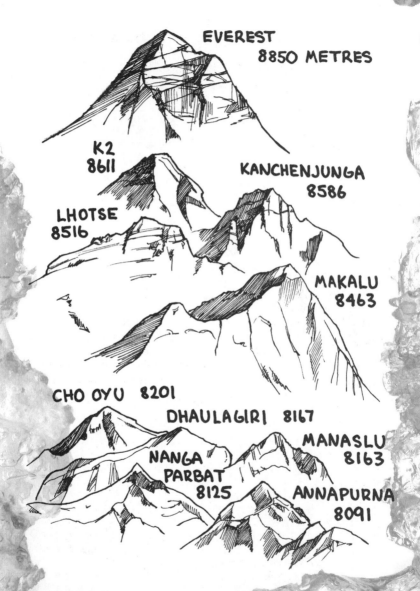

TOP 10

EVEREST
8850 METRES

K2
8611

KANCHENJUNGA
8586

LHOTSE
8516

MAKALU
8463

CHO OYU 8201

DHAULAGIRI 8167

MANASLU
8163

NANGA
PARBAT
8125

ANNAPURNA
8091

11

2

MOUNTAINS CAN KILL!

Some people think climbing a mountain is like walking up a big hill, but mountaineering is incredibly dangerous. Here are some of the ways Everest can kill:

- Avalanche
- Mountain illness
- Falling (in a crevasse or off the mountain)
- Freezing (to death)

Let's look closely at each of these death traps . . .

AVALANCHE

An avalanche is a landslide of snow. Big areas of snow break loose and hurtle down the slope. It can be hard snow that slides like a slab of concrete, or soft light snow that rolls and billows like a huge wave in the surf. You can't outrun (or out-ski or out-snowboard!) it – avalanches have been recorded at speeds of 90 metres per second, which is 320 kilometres per hour (three times faster than your dad drives on the freeway!).

Forty-nine out of 175 deaths on Everest have been as a result of avalanches (that's nearly a third).

What causes an avalanche?

An avalanche can be triggered in several ways. Too much fresh snow can become unstable and simply slide off the mountainside. Loud noises can set one off (so you won't hear any 'cooees' when there's fresh snow on the mountain). Even walking across a snowy slope can start an avalanche, like tearing along a dotted line. At ski resorts patrollers use explosives to cause 'safe' avalanches, so dangerous amounts of snow don't build up.

Can you survive an avalanche?

Yes. Some avalanches are small and easier to avoid. But if you are caught in one, you should 'swim' using a breaststroke action with your arms to try to stay on top of the snow and to clear space in front of your face to breathe. When an avalanche stops, it can set as hard as concrete. You should try to dig an air pocket so you can breathe while people and rescue dogs search for you. Most people who are killed by avalanches are simply in the wrong place at the wrong time.

YETI – THE LEGEND OF BIG FOOT

[CUE: SPOOKY MUSIC] DO DO DO DOO

According to legend, Nepal is the home of the Yeti. Yeti are said to be large human-like mammals with huge feet who usually walk on all fours. Their bodies are covered with thick black or brown fur, and some Sherpas believe Yeti can make themselves invisible. They have a high piercing yell, smell like garlic and live in Nepal up near the snowline. In a temple near Namche Bazaar is a scalp that many locals believed to be the scalp of a Yeti, but in 1960 scientists identified it as a type of antelope, not a Yeti at all. Yet the legend continues . . . In 1984, Australian mountaineers Tim Macartney-Snape and Greg Mortimer found large unexplained footprints near the summit of Mount Everest that some believe were Yeti tracks.

NO SIGN OF A YETI ANYWHERE!

MOUNTAIN ILLNESS

Fresh mountain air can make climbers sick!

Air is made up of oxygen, carbon dioxide and nitrogen. At sea level, these molecules are packed close together, so one breath contains lots of oxygen. In high places, though, the air is thinner so there's less oxygen in every breath you take.

Imagine a room that's so full of balloons you can hardly walk through it. That's what the air is like at sea level, packed with oxygen and other molecules. Now imagine a room that has the same number of balloons in it, but is three times bigger, so they're much more spread out. That's what it's like on the mountain – there is only one-third of the amount of oxygen in the air as there is at sea level.

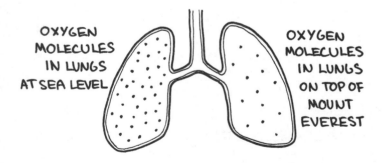

OXYGEN MOLECULES IN LUNGS AT SEA LEVEL

OXYGEN MOLECULES IN LUNGS ON TOP OF MOUNT EVEREST

Just as some people can jump high or run fast and some can't, some people can survive climbing in the thin air but others can't. Many climbers carry extra oxygen tanks on their backs to make breathing easier and safer (although purists consider using extra oxygen cheating!). The lack of oxygen can kill brain cells by the million. The thin air can make people feel dizzy, nauseous and confused. Many, many people have died on mountains as a result of the thin air.

FLAMING EVEREST

The organisers of the 2008 Beijing Olympics are planning for the Olympic torch to go up the southern slopes and down the northern slopes of Mount Everest en route to Beijing. Let's hope the flame doesn't need much oxygen!

Can you survive thin air?

Yes, but it's very hard. The lack of oxygen can make simple tasks, such as putting on boots or lighting a stove, take hours! Oxygen cylinders can help climbers stay warmer, sleep better and breathe more easily while they climb. Most importantly, they give their brains enough oxygen to make sensible decisions. But even with oxygen tanks, climbers over 8000 metres only have the mental skills of a young child. In fact, to think clearly at high altitude, climbers have to stop climbing and rest because there is not enough oxygen to power both their body and their mind!

Climbers have done all sorts of weird things because their brains weren't working properly. Many have started undressing in sub-zero temperatures, and dead bodies are often found with some (or all!) clothes removed. Other climbers have walked off the mountain towards an imaginary path.

The following stories sound funny, but the lack of oxygen at altitude has caused many deaths on Everest.

NOW TO GET THIS UP THE MOUNTAIN!

OXYGEN

MESSING WITH YOUR HEAD

- In 1933 on Mount Everest's North Ridge, British climber Frank Smythe sat for a rest, broke his mint slice in half and offered it to the companion who'd been climbing with him for hours . . . Trouble was, there was no one there! He was alone, as he had been all day.

- In 1978 during a solo climb, Reinhold Messner became aware of an invisible companion directing him through difficult sections. Later, he chatted away to the 'young girl' beside him who told him the weather would hold and he'd reach the summit – and he did.

- In 1988, British climber Stephen Venables was forced to spend a night alone on Everest's South Summit – and he imagined that a lovely old man appeared and rubbed his feet and someone else offered him a hot bath!

- In 1996, Australian Michael Groom felt he was guided by the presence of his dead mate, Lobsang Sherpa. Groom and Lobsang had summitted three years earlier, but Lobsang had fallen and died on the way down.

FALLING

Mount Everest is not the place for clumsy climbers. Some sections are more dangerous than others – especially the infamous Khumbu Icefall, also known as 'Suicide Passage' and 'Hellfire Alley'. The Icefall is made up of huge towers of ice. Climbers have to walk across ladder bridges over crevasses which can be as deep as 35 metres. A fall could kill, or it may be impossible to climb out of the crevasse . . . To make it even trickier, crevasses change with the snow conditions. One day there might be an area of firm flat snow, the next there's a crazily deep crevasse.

Falling into a crevasse isn't the only problem. Things can also fall *on* you. In 1996, a young Sherpa was killed by a boulder that rolled down the mountain. Several people have also been killed by falling seracs – enormous blocks of ice (imagine one the size of a car!) that melt, break off and fall on top of you.

Then, of course, *you* could fall off the mountain. If you were to slip off the summit ridge, it's more than two kilometres straight down!

Can you survive without falling (or something falling on you)?

Often climbers are clipped into ropes that will (hopefully!) hold them if they fall and start to slide thousands of metres down the icy mountain. Climbers minimise the danger by making good choices, such as clipping into safety ropes where possible, and not climbing in unstable areas during the hot part of the day when melting snow might dislodge boulders or make seracs topple. Of the people who've died on Everest, forty-nine (nearly a third) were killed by a fall and eight died because something fell on them.

HANG ON! I'LL PULL YOU UP!

FREEZING

Last but definitely not least, the cold air is also a killer.
Think of how warm a 25°C (degrees Celsius) day feels.
Now think of how cold a freezer feels at minus 2°C.
Well, on the summit of Everest, it's often minus 40°C!
And that's just the air temperature. If it's windy, it can
feel like minus 55°C.

Why? Windchill factor! When it's cold but there's no
wind, your body heats up the layer of air closest to your
skin, so you're not quite so cold. But if there's wind,
it blows that layer of warmer air away and . . . brrrr!

If you could stick a thermometer inside your
body (please don't), the temperature would read 37°C.
If your body temperature falls even a tiny bit below
this, you start to shiver, which is your body's way of
warming you up. If your body temperature keeps
falling to 35°C, you have a condition called
hypothermia.

Climbers who have hypothermia might be clumsy,
have slurred speech, do something silly, or feel tired
and sleepy. (They might even want to lie down in the

snow.) At 32°C, their body stops shivering – it's run out of energy – and they're in real trouble. They often curl up and fall unconscious. At 28°C or colder, they are pale, waxy, and won't blink even if you punch them. Often, at this point, their heart will stop. Uh oh.

THE JETSTREAM

The layer of wind that whips around Earth from east to west at an incredible speed is called a jetstream. At certain times of year, the jetstream drops to an altitude of about 7500 metres and blasts the upper slopes of the world's highest mountains. The wind is so loud, climbers can't hear each other over it, even if they yell. At the top of Mount Everest there are only a few weeks of the year (around May) when the jetstream eases enough so as not to blow a human off the mountain.

Can you survive the cold?

Sure, it sounds bad, but wearing the right clothes and knowing how to stay warm can prevent hypothermia. (Read more about clothing on page 48.)

FREEZING FACTS

AIR TEMPERATURE	WHAT HAPPENS
25°C	a naked person starts to feel cool
12°C	your fingers become clumsier and numb
8°C	you're less sensitive to pain
0°C	your skin starts to freeze (frostnip)
–5°C	the tissue beneath your skin can freeze (frostbite)
–25°C	any bare skin will instantly go white, because it's so cold that bloods stops flowing to that bit of your body
–30°C	if bare skin touches metal, it could get stuck there.*
–50°C	bare skin freezes in a minute, your eyelashes freeze your eyelids shut, the surface of your eye can freeze over, lumps of frozen breath form like icicles on a man's beard
–55°C	bare skin freezes in 30 seconds. When you exhale, your breath turns into crackling ice crystals as it comes out of your mouth – this is known as 'whispering of the stars'. The inside of your lungs could freeze.
–89°C	the lowest temperature ever recorded on Earth, in 1983 at the Russian research station Vostok on the Antarctic icecap
–220°C	the temperature on the surface of Pluto

* The solution, according to the notes of one Antarctic expedition, is to 'urinate on the affected part as the warm urine will melt the ice and release the hand unharmed'. Nice!

COUGH YOUR
HEART OUT

T. H. Somervell climbed Mount Everest with his
friend Edward Norton in 1922. He reported:
'When darkness was gathering I had one of my fits
of coughing and dislodged something in my throat
that stuck so that I could neither breathe in nor out.
I could not . . . make a sign to Norton or stop him,
so I sat down in the snow to die while he walked
on. I made one or two attempts to breathe . . . finally
I pressed my chest with both hands, gave one last
almighty push – and the obstruction came up.'

The obstruction was part of his frozen lungs. Yuk!

3

AIMING TOO HIGH?

Given all the dangers involved in climbing Everest, the early expeditioners were truly extraordinary. One of the most famous was George Mallory.

AMAZING ATTEMPTS ON EVEREST

Even when he was growing up in England, Mallory loved to climb. He climbed every tree his sister ever dared him to, no matter how high. He was such a good athlete and climber, he was selected for the first-ever expedition to Everest in 1921, and the next in 1922.

In both these expeditions, he proved to be an excellent team member: energetic, hardworking, caring towards other people (particularly the Sherpas) and by far the best climber. But he wasn't perfect. He was considered reckless and very forgetful. He was also a little eccentric, sometimes striding around the lower altitudes stark naked, wearing only his boots and backpack!

Mallory and his team-mates found a route up the mountain and in 1921 reached a record height of 7010 metres. In 1922 they made it even higher, to 8170 metres, just 680 metres below the summit. It was an epic day in which they climbed in the dark, carrying candles to avoid crevasses. Mallory's team reached these incredible heights without modern oxygen tanks or climbing equipment, and wearing very basic clothing. They had on woollen jumpers, tweed jackets, silk underwear, pith helmets, several pairs of socks and hobnailed boots!

QUOTABLE QUOTE

A reporter once asked Mallory why he wanted so badly to get to the summit of Mount Everest. His answer became as famous as him: he said, 'Because it's there.'

THIRD TIME UNLUCKY

As the star climber, Mallory was invited on a third expedition to Mount Everest in 1924. Although he really wanted to reach the summit, he now knew how dangerous it was and how much he would miss his wife Ruth and their three children. He promised Ruth that if he made it to the summit, he would put a photo of her there. He confided to his friend Geoffrey Keynes, 'This is going to be more like war than mountaineering – I don't expect to come back.'

Sadly, he was right.

The 1924 expedition was a tough one from the start. The leader died of malaria during the trek across Tibet. (At that time the Nepalese king still wouldn't let them into Nepal.) Heavy snowfalls forced them to retreat down the mountain, and two Sherpas died of frostbite and altitude sickness.

The new leader, Edward Norton, reached an amazing height of 8573 metres (only 277 metres below the summit!) without oxygen, but he'd forgotten his sunglasses and became snow blind.

Back at camp, lying in his tent, Norton decided it was time for them all to go home, but Mallory asked for one more chance at the summit. Exhausted and blind, Norton agreed.

SNOW BLINDNESS

Even at 3000 metres the sun's UV rays are 50 per cent stronger than at sea level. Add to that the reflection off the bright white snow and snow blindness becomes a big risk for climbers. If they forget to wear their sunglasses, they can become painfully blind six to 12 hours after they 'burn' their eyes. Luckily, it's usually temporary.

I CAN'T SEE! I CAN'T SEE!!!

On 8 June 1924 Mallory set out with a young Oxford student named Andrew 'Sandy' Irvine. Mallory carried a photo of Ruth, and Irvine carried the Kodak Vest Pocket camera they hoped to use to prove to the world they had made the summit.

Noel Odell was a climber at a lower camp. At 12.50 p.m. he caught glimpses through the clouds of Mallory and Irvine climbing. He wrote in his diary:

'The summit ridge and final peak of Everest was unveiled. My eyes became fixed on one tiny black spot silhouetted . . . beneath a rock step. The black spot moved. Another became apparent and moved up the snow to join the other on the crest . . . Then the whole fascinating vision vanished, enveloped in cloud once more.'

That was the last time anyone saw Mallory and Irvine alive. The other expeditioners waited for hours, then Odell went searching for them. At their highest camp he discovered that forgetful Mallory had left his torch in his tent. After two days, Odell laid the camp blankets out in a cross to send a message to Base Camp that Mallory and Irvine were dead.

DID MALLORY AND IRVINE MAKE IT?

The question is: did Mallory and Irvine reach the summit before they died? No one is really sure.

Odell saw them on a ridge called Second Step, which isn't far from the summit. And in 1933,

Irvine's ice-axe was found nearby. In 1975, Chinese climber Wang Hangbao saw a body in old-fashioned clothing on the North Face, not far below the summit.

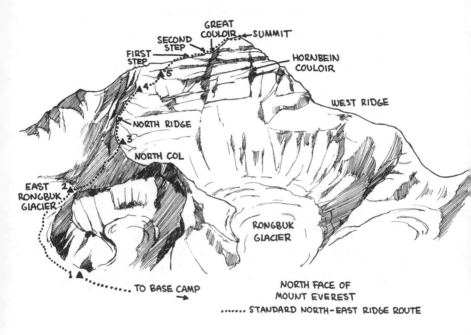

NORTH FACE OF MOUNT EVEREST

.... STANDARD NORTH-EAST RIDGE ROUTE

Then, in 1999 (a low snow year), a group of climbers organised an expedition to search for Andrew Irvine's body and the Kodak Vest Pocket camera he had carried. Kodak said that, even though the film was 75 years old, they would probably be able to develop it to see if it showed photos taken from the summit.

The searchers started on the North Face and after only two hours they found a dead body lying face down, head uphill, partly covered by gravel. The man's lower body had been pecked at by birds, but his upper back was bare and perfectly white where layers of shirts and woollen jumpers had been torn away. His arms were above his head, fingers still grabbing into the loose rocks as if he'd tried to stop himself from sliding. He had a rope tied around his waist, but it had broken when he fell – and so had one leg. He was still wearing his hobnailed boots.

Beside the body, one of the searchers started to carve Irvine's gravestone while another looked at the clothing labels. Suddenly he said, 'It's not Irvine!' The labels read 'G. Mallory'. They had found the famous man himself, 75 years after he died.

Before the climbers buried Mallory's body under rocks, they checked his pockets and found sun goggles, an altimeter, a pocket-knife and some letters. But there was no photo of his wife Ruth.

Had he made the summit and put the photo there? Was he the first man to stand on the summit of Mount Everest? Without Irvine's body (or, more importantly, the camera he was carrying) we'll probably never know.

AIR AND FEATHERS

On the 1922 expedition with Mallory was an Australian called George Finch. He was an excellent climber and an 'ideas man'. One night during a gale he rigged up the oxygen tanks in the tents so everyone could breathe more easily while they rested. Today, nearly all climbers follow his idea. Finch was also the first to make a feather-filled doona into a jacket. Some of his team-mates thought he was being silly, but it proved to be much warmer than wool and tweed jackets. In fact, down jackets like the one he made are still worn by climbers today.

COMING!

PRESERVED BODIES

There are two main reasons why Mallory's body was mostly intact so many years after he died:

- The environment on Mount Everest is too harsh for most body-eating bacteria to survive.

- In the same way a freezer keeps steaks in good condition, the freezing temperature on Mount Everest preserves the bodies of climbers who die on its slopes.

There are at least 41 dead bodies on the northern slopes of Mount Everest alone and often climbers have to step over them! Many climbers believe that lugging a dead body down the mountain is too great a risk. It took 12 people eight hours to get a Taiwanese climber's body through the Khumbu Icefall, which is only 600 metres long. Sherpas believe dead climbers become ghosts on the mountain so they don't like to touch them. Where possible, bodies are moved off the trail or lowered into a crevasse. If they are below the snowline, they are covered with a pile of stones.

4

DESTINATION BASE CAMP

Not many climbers make it all the way up Mount Everest, but hundreds of people each year travel to Everest Base Camp, the first step on the way to the summit.

COLOURFUL KATHMANDU

Today, the easiest way to get to Everest Base Camp is to fly to Kathmandu (*Cat-man-doo*), the capital city of Nepal. Kathmandu is home to a mix of religions and cultures. The city is crowded with carved temples, hairy gurus with way-out body piercings, and lots of cows.

Yes, cows. Cows are sacred to the Hindu religion, so they're free to wander around the city. And if it pleases them to stand in the middle of the road and cause a humungous traffic jam and lots of angry tooting, they will!

For climbers, Kathmandu is an important stopover. It's a place to buy a trekking permit, food and equipment. Many people hire a guiding company there to organise the paperwork and supplies, and to take them to the summit of Mount Everest. A guiding company can charge as much as $65 000 per person. Phew! If you want to stand on the top of the world one day – start saving that pocket money!

ONWARDS AND UPWARDS TO BASE CAMP

From Kathmandu, most climbers take a small plane to a mountain village called Lukla. Landing at the little airstrip can be scary – the runway is on a huge uphill slant with a steep mountain face at the end of it (and lots of crashed planes!). Lukla used to have only a few houses, where Sherpas grazed yaks (Himalayan relatives of the cow) and grew a few crops, but now it is full of lodges, hotels and restaurants. From here, it takes nine days to walk to Base Camp, carrying backpacks. There are no roads up the mountain.

Climbers can't rush to Base Camp anyway – they need time for their bodies to get used to the high altitude. Lukla is about 3000 metres above sea level. Most Australians live at sea level, so at an altitude of 3000 metres they may find they're tired and panting a lot because of the thin air. Climbers drink a lot of water and walk at a steady pace, and their bodies gradually adjust.

On the trail from Lukla to Base Camp each day, there are beautiful views and smiling local people carrying heavy loads of groceries, drinks or firewood balanced on their heads. Visitors quickly learn to get off the trail when they hear the bells that hang around the necks of hairy yaks. The only road rule yaks know is to stay on the track, and everything on two legs gets out of their way!

The villages along the way are Phakding, Namche Bazaar (which has a fantastic market), Tengpoche (a famous monastery for Buddhist monks), Pheriche (the first-aid post), Lobuche and finally Gorak Shep – the last village before Base Camp. Climbers stay in guesthouses where there are beds but no showers, so they have to wash in a bucket. (Well, not actually *in* a bucket.) The local food is usually dal bhat (*darl bart*) – lentil soup with rice. They don't drink the water unless it's been boiled, or they'd be stuck on the toilet for days, and the toilets are very, very basic – raised wooden platforms with holes in them perched over mounds of frozen poo . . . yuk!

The trek to Base Camp winds between the biggest

mountains in the world along a river of ice called the Khumbu Glacier. The glacier moves very slowly – between 45 and 400 metres a year. But where it flows around a corner or into rocks, the ice slowly piles up to create huge, weird ice sculptures in the Khumbu Icefall and Phantom Alley.

BASE CAMP AT LAST!

At an altitude of 5400 metres, climbers finally reach Base Camp. There's a sea of colourful tents with each

expedition group flying its own flag. People chat in the sunshine and drink cups of tea, or work on equipment, while others carry big packs as they head off to start climbing the mountain. So long as there is no wind blowing, it's warm in the sunshine and some people wear T-shirts, even though they're surrounded by ice and snow. Everyone slaps on lots of sunscreen. The thin air here means you get sunburnt very easily.

TENT CITY ~ BASICS AT BASE CAMP

The largest tent for each expedition is the mess tent, where the climbers eat. It has a kitchen with fold-up tables and small chairs, boxes of food, gas cookers and solar-powered lights. Nearby is the communications tent where the satellite phone is kept. There might be a shower in a tiny tent – just a rubber hose attached to a tank. The toilets are in tents too, quite a walk away because the smell's pretty gross. At the end of the climbing season, the rubbish, including toilet tanks, is carried back to Namche Bazaar, to keep the mountain as clean as possible. (Ew, not a nice job!)

As the sun goes behind the peaks, the temperature drops to below freezing. People retreat to their sleeping tents where special mattresses keep them off the ice, warm and cosy in their down sleeping bags. Lying on a river of ice, climbers can hear the crash of avalanches falling down the surrounding mountains as well as the spooky creaks, cracks and groans of the glacier as it moves underneath their tents.

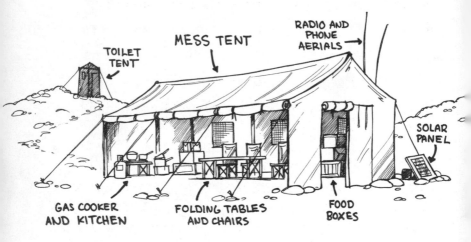

RADIO AND PHONE AERIALS →

MESS TENT

TOILET TENT

SOLAR PANEL

GAS COOKER AND KITCHEN

FOLDING TABLES AND CHAIRS

FOOD BOXES

WHAT'S ON THE MENU?

Climbers need loads of high-energy food because the cold, the altitude and the exercise mean they burn zillions of kilojoules. Even if they eat well, most people go home from an expedition five to ten kilograms lighter than when they started! The altitude often reduces hunger. This might be because so much blood flows to the limbs to prevent frostbite that there's less blood around the stomach, which makes it less active. So at Base Camp there's plenty of tempting chocolate, soup, cheese, eggs, tuna, pasta, porridge, rice, and local vegetables such as lentils, potatoes, corn and barley.

SLOW COOKING

At sea level, water boils when it's heated to 100 degrees Celsius. As you get higher, water boils at a lower temperature. It's the heat in the water that cooks food, not whether it's boiling or not, so the higher you are, the longer it takes to heat food hot enough to cook. At Base Camp, water boils at 85 degrees Celsius, and food takes seven times as long to cook – unless you have a pressure cooker!

PASTA'S READY!

WHO DOES WHAT?

Guide: a climbing leader who helps you with your equipment and getting up the mountain

Sherpa: the local Sherpa people have lived in the valleys of the Himalayas for many generations. They are already used to the high altitude, and herding yaks up the huge grassy hills and planting and digging up potatoes makes them strong and fit. Sherpas are often employed on climbing expeditions as porters, cooks or guides.

Sirdar: the head Sherpa in each expedition, very experienced and respected

Porter: helps carry food and equipment up and down the valley

Base Camp manager: makes sure there's enough food, equipment and medicine for everyone on the expedition and oversees the smooth running of your Base Camp home

Cook: in charge of whipping up great food at Base Camp, even if you're not very hungry because of the altitude!

Cook's assistant: often a young Sherpa who, if you're lucky, will bring you hot sweet tea to drink in the morning when you're still in your sleeping bag

SMALL STEPS TO THE SUMMIT

Walking can be hard work due to the thin air, so climbers can't rush straight up Everest. First they walk around Base Camp very slowly. Their first hike is to Camp 1 (the first of up to eight camps on the way to the summit) then back to Base Camp. Then they hike to Camp 2, and so on. Sound tough? That's why it took so long for someone to do it for the first time! Today, there is more than one route from Base Camp to the summit – but all are incredibly difficult and many climbers do not survive the journey.

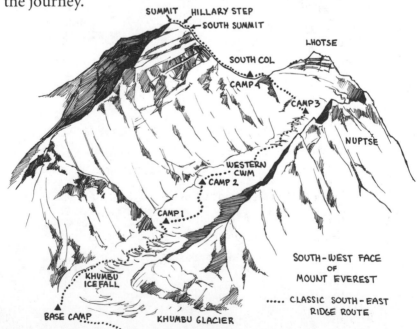

SUMMIT · HILLARY STEP
SOUTH SUMMIT
LHOTSE
SOUTH COL
CAMP 4
CAMP 3
NUPTSE
WESTERN CWM
CAMP 2
CAMP 1
KHUMBU ICEFALL
BASE CAMP
KHUMBU GLACIER

SOUTH-WEST FACE
OF
MOUNT EVEREST

····· CLASSIC SOUTH-EAST
RIDGE ROUTE

KEEPING THE COLD OUT

Climbing Mount Everest requires special clothing to keep the cold out – and special equipment to help you make it safely to the summit (and back). You'll need an ice-axe, harness, oxygen tank and crampons.

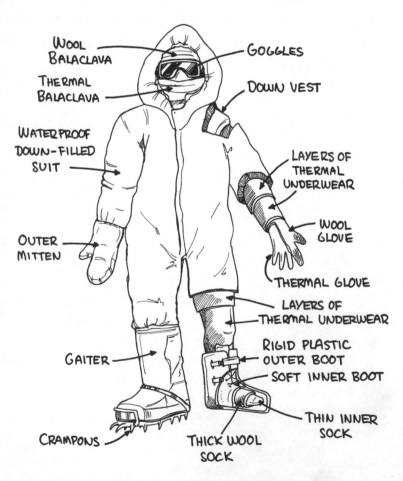

WOOL BALACLAVA

GOGGLES

THERMAL BALACLAVA

DOWN VEST

WATERPROOF DOWN-FILLED SUIT

LAYERS OF THERMAL UNDERWEAR

WOOL GLOVE

OUTER MITTEN

THERMAL GLOVE

LAYERS OF THERMAL UNDERWEAR

RIGID PLASTIC OUTER BOOT

SOFT INNER BOOT

GAITER

THIN INNER SOCK

CRAMPONS

THICK WOOL SOCK

Mountaineers started using crampons in the early 1900s to help them grip on slippery ice. Crampons are metal frames with sharp, pointy spikes for digging into snow and ice. The frames clip onto the bottom of your boots, and can be unclipped when you are climbing on rocks or just walking around camp. Walking with crampons can be tricky at first, and takes some getting used to!

You'll also need a backpack to carry extra clothes, water, food, an oxygen tank and mask, sleeping bag, first-aid kit, knife, head torch, batteries and a camera.

FROSTY FINGERS

Sixteen-year-old Sherpa Temba Tsheri – who once held the record for being the youngest person to reach the summit – took his gloves off high on the mountain, to tie his shoelaces. It took him 45 minutes to do this, by which time frostbite had set in. When he got down from the summit, he had to have five fingers amputated.

5

THE RACE TO
THE SUMMIT

After Mallory and Norton and the other heroes of
the 1920s got so close, it took almost 30 years for the
race to the summit to finally be won. Why so long?
Well, there was the huge cost of expeditions, and the
difficulty of getting permission to enter from the
Nepalese king. Also, many of the best young climbers
were killed (or at least busy fighting) in World War II.

The British, in particular, were desperate to be
first to climb the highest mountain on Earth. The race
to reach the North Pole was won by American Robert
Peary in 1909 and the race to reach the South Pole was

won in 1911 by Norwegian Roald Amundsen (five weeks ahead of the British team led by Robert F. Scott). So the British were very keen to be the first to reach what they called 'the Third Pole' – the highest point on the planet.

KEEPING THE DREAM ALIVE

In 1950 the Chinese invaded Tibet and closed the old route to Everest from Tibet. But as one door closed, another one opened – the King of Nepal began to let foreigners explore his beautiful country. At about this time, a young Tibetan man called Tenzing Norgay (which means 'the fortunate one') fell in love with mountain climbing.

Meanwhile Michael Ward, a young surgeon in London, was spending his spare time at the Royal

Geographical Society studying maps and photos of Everest. One day, he came across a photo taken by a Spitfire pilot at the end of the war. It showed what everyone had hoped for: a possible new route to the summit. And it was in Nepal . . .

Ward gathered his friends for an expedition and, at the last moment, asked the famous mountaineer and explorer Eric Shipton to be their leader. Shipton invited two young New Zealand climbers – Earle Riddiford and Edmund Hillary.

In 1951, Shipton's expedition explored Ward's route up the South-east Ridge and found a way through the icy jungle now known as the Khumbu Icefall. They planned to return in 1952, but that year the Nepalese government allowed only one expedition to visit Everest – a Swiss expedition guided by Sherpa Tenzing Norgay.

THE SWISS ATTEMPT – 1952

While the British chewed their fingernails at home, the Swiss climbers and their Sherpa team worked their way up Everest's new route. After climbing through the

dangerous Khumbu Icefall they were the first humans
to set foot on the Lhotse Glacier and to climb as far
as a ridge between two peaks named South Col. Here,
7860 metres above sea level, the temperature can fall to
minus 40°C. The wind is so loud that climbers have to
shout to be heard by the person standing next to them!
Tents flap so fast, they sound like gunfire.

By this stage, frostbite and mountain illness had made nearly all the Sherpas turn back. Only one Sherpa remained – Tenzing Norgay. He and three of the Swiss climbers pressed on, but without the other Sherpas to help they had to leave much of their equipment behind. They could carry only one tent.

By late afternoon, they had reached 8382 metres. As the sun started to set, two of the Swiss climbers agreed to go back down to South Col, while Tenzing Norgay and Raymond Lambert stayed the night in the tent on the ridge in order to try for the summit in the morning. Imagine how scary that night would have been: it was minus 40 degrees and they had no sleeping bags and no stove (so the only drink they had was some ice they'd melted with a candle). One decent puff of wind would have blown them and their tent off the mountain. They couldn't sleep, but it was safer to stay awake anyway, as hypothermia could have killed them.

After a long, freezing, fearful night the sun came up, the clouds rolled in and the weather got worse. Lambert and Tenzing struggled on to a point only 240 metres below the summit but, utterly exhausted, they made the tough decision to turn back. Mount Everest was still unclimbed . . .

THE BRITISH ATTEMPT ~ 1953

The British team were elated by the failure of the Swiss expedition. They knew 1953 was probably their last chance to win the race to the top as the Nepalese government had promised a permit to the French for 1954 and the Swiss for 1955.

The British hired a new leader, army colonel John Hunt, who was a good climber and an excellent organiser. He made sure the new team did an incredible amount of preparation. Meanwhile, Tenzing wrote to Hunt to say he had recovered from the Swiss expedition. Hunt happily offered him a position as climber and sirdar – head Sherpa of the expedition.

The team practised with new oxygen equipment,

had special high-altitude boots made, and ordered aluminium ladders to help them through the Khumbu Icefall. (This was all considered very high-tech at the time!) Hunt made detailed plans of who would carry what in their packs, and then all the equipment was

packed in crates and shipped to India.

The British climbers spent one month sailing to India on the *Stratheden*, days and days on a dusty, hot train to Nepal, and finally gathered in Kathmandu. They were ready to go. Except they had to wait – Edmund Hillary was still in New Zealand helping his beekeeper father with his bees!

When Hillary finally arrived, the team began the three-week walk to the mountain. With so much

equipment they had to employ 350 Nepalese porters (men and women) who each carried a load of 27 kilograms for 17 days. They also had to hire an extra 12 porters to carry all the coins needed to pay the porters!

LOST IN TRANSLATION

One of the toughest porters was 13-year-old Sherpa Mingma who carried heavy loads that would have been difficult for a grown man. But his English did cause some problems. One day, the team's doctor asked him to carry a box of test tubes to Camp 3. After hours of trekking, Mingma arrived carrying a box of jars of mango chutney!

After the long walk to the mountain and another three weeks getting used to the thin air at Thyangboche Monastery, the team was feeling strong and excited. They reached the dreaded Khumbu Icefall 12 days faster than the Swiss had the year before, and they were in much better physical condition. Hunt's plan was on track.

Of course, there were challenges. One day, coming down through the Icefall, Hillary decided to use his very long legs to leap across a crevasse instead of crawling across the ladder. As he landed, the ice gave way beneath him and he began to fall. Luckily, there was a jerk around his waist and he hung from the safety rope with his heart thumping while the ice shelf crashed down to the bottom of the crevasse. He was saved by the quick thinking of his rope partner that day – Tenzing Norgay.

Hillary and Tenzing were a good team from the start. Tenzing said of Hillary, 'A wonderful climber . . . [who] had great strength and endurance. Like many men of action, he didn't talk much, but he was nevertheless a fine and cheerful companion; and he was popular with the Sherpas because, in things like food and equipment, he always shared whatever he had.'

Both men were very strong at high altitudes, excellent mountaineers, and both were incredibly determined.

After most of the equipment had been carried through the Icefall and up to the Western Cwm*, John Hunt selected two teams who would attempt the summit. Team one, Charles Evans and Tom Bourdillon, used a new oxygen system. Team two, Tenzing Norgay and Edmund Hillary, used the old oxygen system that previous expeditions had used. Hunt, Alfred Gregory and five Sherpas went with them as far as South Col.

The first team set out for the summit on 26 May 1953. Bourdillon and Evans made great time while their new equipment was working properly. By 1 p.m. they were standing higher than anyone had ever stood before – 8750 metres! But Evans was having trouble with his oxygen system – he could hardly breathe and

---

* Cwm is pronounced 'coom'. It was named by Mallory and is Welsh for valley.

he was getting dangerously exhausted. The two were so close to the summit, but they didn't want to die . . . so they headed back to the camp at South Col.

Hillary recalled:

'They moved silently towards us – a few stiff, jerky paces – they stop. A few more paces. They were very near to complete exhaustion . . . from head to foot they were encased with ice. There was ice on their clothing, on their oxygen sets and on their rope. It was hanging from their beards and eyebrows. They must have had the most terrible time in the wind and snow.'

Hillary and Tenzing were the expedition's last chance . . .

DEATH-DEFYING
MOUNTAIN-TAMERS

Mountaineers trust their climbing partners with their lives, so they need to be sure they climb with the right kind of person. Here are some characteristics that make a great mountaineer:

Mountaineers are very fit and have strong lungs and hearts, and blood that carries lots of oxygen efficiently. Edmund Hillary had an amazingly efficient body at high altitude. He could climb comfortably in the thin air while other people puffed and stumbled and wheezed. Some people get altitude sickness at 2500 metres, yet he could function well at three times that height!

Mountaineers are technically prepared and well-practised with their equipment – crampons, ice-axes and climbing ropes. George Mallory was particularly quick with his ice-axe. Once, when he was leading three friends down Mount Everest, the person last in line slipped and started sliding down the mountain. The four climbers were roped together so the rope pulled the third man and then the second man down the mountain towards Mallory. With only seconds to think, Mallory wrapped one arm around the rope, and with the other he dug his ice-axe deep into the snow and held on very, very tight.

Even though his friends were big men and sliding quickly, Mallory and his ice-axe managed to hold on and save all four of them from sliding thousands of metres down the mountain to certain death.

Mountaineers make sensible, unselfish decisions. They don't put their own life, or anyone else's, in danger unnecessarily. John Hunt desperately wanted to climb to the top of Mount Everest. But he made a good unselfish decision and selected the best teams for the job – which didn't include him.

Most of all, mountaineers respect the mountain. They are very aware that the mountain can kill, so they know to be prepared and respectful. Anyone who gets to the summit should be proud – and should also know they've been blessed (or very lucky!).

YES, YES, YOU'RE VERY CLEVER. BUT WHAT PRECISELY DO WE DO NOW?

6

THE TOP
OF THE WORLD!

Hillary and Tenzing set off on the morning of 28 May 1953 with George Lowe, Alfred Gregory and Sherpa Ang Nyima each carrying 18 kilograms of equipment for them. (Hunt had selflessly decided to help the exhausted Bourdillon down to Base Camp.) Hillary and Tenzing carried 23 kilograms each. Imagine, that's like lugging 23 cartons of milk up a very steep hill while you can hardly breathe!

When the others left Hillary and Tenzing on a tiny ice shelf at 8500 metres, the pair was feeling strong. They set up camp, ate their rations and drank plenty of hot lemon tea. They had sleeping bags, a Primus stove and oxygen to breathe through the night – completely different to Tenzing's experience the year before.

They dozed through the night, and at 4 a.m. prepared a breakfast of hot lemon and sugar, with tinned sardines on biscuits. Hillary had forgotten to put his boots in his sleeping bag and they were frozen solid so he heated them over the stove until they were soft enough to wear. They then put on every piece of clothing they had, including three pairs of gloves (silk, wool and windproof) and headed out into the snow. It was 6.30 a.m. on the biggest day of their lives.

By 8 a.m. they'd found some oxygen cylinders Bourdillon and Evans had left behind in the snow. By 9 a.m. they had reached the South Summit and set out along the dangerous Summit Ridge, where no one had ever stepped before. Snow and ice curled over the narrow ridge. One wrong step on unsupported snow and Hillary and Tenzing would be hurtling down the slope (two kilometres straight down).

They crept along the ridge, sinking knee-deep in snow at every step, before looking up to see one

final hurdle: a 12-metre-high cliff of rock and ice!
This must have been an awful moment for them . . .
It looked almost impossible to climb. Then Hillary
spotted a crack between the rock and the ice and
jammed his foot, and then his tall body, into it. If the
ice had cracked, he would have been sliding down the
mountain and almost definitely dead. But it, and his
luck, held as he levered his way up to come out on top,
panting and exhausted. Tenzing followed. This last
obstacle is now called the Hillary Step.

THE VIEW THROUGH THIN AIR

The thin air at the summit of Everest
means you can see much further than
you can at sea level. It's so close to space
(where there's no oxygen) that from the top
of Mount Everest the sky looks black – even
in the middle of the day. Oxygen in the
atmosphere is what makes the sky appear
blue from sea level.

Roped together, they moved along the knife-sharp ridge again, step by careful step, with Hillary using his ice-axe to cut steps in the snow.

'*We seemed to go on forever, tired now . . . I looked right and there was a rounded snowy dome . . . Next moment I had moved on to an exposed area of snow with nothing but space in every direction. Tenzing joined me and . . . we realised we were on top of the world! It was 11.30 a.m. on 29 May 1953. In typical Anglo-Saxon fashion I stretched out my arm for a handshake, but this was not enough for Tenzing, who threw his arms around my shoulders in a mighty hug!*'

In the 15 minutes they spent on the summit, the pair looked for evidence of Mallory and Irvine but found nothing. Far below, Tenzing could see where he had tended yaks as a young boy, and where he'd worked on his first expedition. He buried sweets his daughter

Nima had given him as a gift to the gods, and said a Tibetan prayer of thanks: '*Tuji Chey, Chomolungma*', meaning 'I am grateful, Chomolungma'. Meanwhile, Hillary buried a crucifix given to Hunt by a priest in his village in England. They ate some mint cake, then took photos all around the ridge as proof, including a shot of Tenzing flying the flags of the United Nations, Great Britain, Nepal and India. Then they started the dangerous climb down to tell their wonderful news.

FREEZE FRAME

There are no photos of Hillary on the summit. Hillary said, 'Tenzing was not much of a photographer and the summit was no place to start teaching him.' Hillary also confessed that after showing his respect to the mountain, he had no choice but to pee on it! He'd had a lot of hot lemon to drink at breakfast . . .

SPREADING THE NEWS

Hillary and Tenzing passed their overnight camp at 2 p.m. Many hours later they were relieved to see George Lowe climbing to their South Col camp to meet them with hot soup and emergency oxygen. It was not a second too soon – Hillary's oxygen ran out as he reached his tent at South Col.

No radio could transmit from South Col to Base Camp, so they told their story to Lowe and Wilfrid Noyce, and for one night they were the only four people in the world who knew Mount Everest had been climbed.

The next day Hunt watched anxiously from the lower camp on the Western Cwm as the summit team plodded slowly and wearily towards him. Then Lowe couldn't hide it any longer: he held up a thumb and raised his ice-axe to point at the summit . . . Suddenly, everyone started running towards the team. Hunt rushed up and threw his arms around Hillary and Tenzing with tears rolling down his face. The expedition had been a success. It was a dream come true for them all.

TEAM PHOTO

Members of the 1953 Mount Everest Expedition Team can be seen in this photo, with porters seated in front, including Sherpas **Ang Nyima** (22), **Dawa Thondup** (49) and **Ang Tsering** (16).

In the back row, from left to right, are:
Tom Stobart (39), filmmaker; **Dawa Tenzing** (46), Sherpa;
Charles Evans (33), surgeon and deputy leader; **Charles Wylie** (32), Gurkha officer and in charge of equipment; **Edmund Hillary** (33), beekeeper; **John Hunt** (42), army colonel and expedition leader; **Tenzing Norgay** (38), Sherpa sirdar; **George Lowe** (28), school teacher; **Michael Ward** (28), doctor; **Tom Bourdillon** (28), rocket scientist; **George Band** (23), university student; **Griffith Pugh** (44), physiologist; **Alfred Gregory** (39), travel agent; **Wilfrid Noyce** (34), schoolmaster and writer.

Not pictured are **Michael Westmacott** (27), statistician, **James Morris** (27), *Times* journalist, and Sherpa **Nawang Gombu** (17), Tenzing Norgay's nephew.

THE CROWNING SUCCESS

On 30 May 1953, Hillary and Tenzing told their story to journalist James Morris, who realised that young Princess Elizabeth was to be crowned Queen of England in three days. Morris climbed as quickly as possible back through the Icefall to Base Camp and prepared a message in code. The *Times* broke the story in London on the morning of the coronation: 'Glorious Coronation Day news! Everest – Everest the unconquerable – has been conquered . . .'

THE NEWS OF THE SUCCESSFUL CLIMB WAS GREETED WITH SCENES OF WILD ANGLO-SAXON EXCITEMENT AT BASE CAMP...

7

BECAUSE IT'S THERE

Since 1953, more than 1100 people have made it to the summit of Mount Everest. Over 175 of them died before they made it back down. That's one in six – so, if you and your five best friends set out to climb Mount Everest and all six of you reached the summit, the odds are that one of you would die on the way down. But some people thrive on extreme adventure, and to them the risk of death makes it even more exciting.

DEATH AT THE TOP OF THE WORLD

In 1996 eight people died on Mount Everest in a single day, including New Zealand expedition leader Rob Hall. Rob had stayed behind to help an American climber, Doug Hansen, who had reached the summit but was exhausted and suffering from mountain illness. Before dying of hypothermia near South Summit, Rob was patched via radio through to his home phone in New Zealand so he could say goodbye to his pregnant wife.

Michael Groom from Queensland was one of the guides on the mountain that day. His strength and leadership saved several lives. Among those he helped rescue was American Beck Weathers, who was so badly frostbitten that he later had to have both hands amputated. He probably would have died if not for a brave helicopter pilot, Lieutenant Colonel Madan Khatri Chhetri of the Nepalese army, who risked his life flying above the Khumbu Icefall to rescue him. At the time, it was the highest ever helicopter rescue. The air is so thin, it's a wonder the chopper didn't fall out of the sky!

CHOPPERS ON THE MOUNTAIN

At the time of the helicopter rescue of 1996, the highest altitude at which helicopters could land was 6000 metres. Weathers's rescue was at an amazing 6053 metres. The chopper was stripped down to reduce weight, and could carry only one passenger. White snow makes it even more dangerous – it's hard to see where to land a helicopter on a snowy mountain. That day, a famous American climber and cinematographer, David Breashears, was there with his IMAX team. They had an excellent idea. They sprinkled red cordial in a big 'X' on the snow to mark where the helicopter could safely land.

ANY MORE CORDIAL ANYONE?

Hello Pilot could you please land your helicop...

Technology has improved since then. In 2005, a specially designed helicopter landed on the summit of Mount Everest!

But the 1996 tragedy made guiding companies think long and hard about whether it was too dangerous to take inexperienced climbers up Mount Everest. Now, the guiding companies have rules that everyone has to follow which make it safer for less skilled climbers. However many precations you take, mountaineering remains dangerous. In fact, it is an adventure and an achievement because it's *not* safe – something that's hard to forget when you remember all the people whose final resting place is the slopes of Everest.

HIGH SACRIFICE

In 2004, British computer expert Conan Harrod was waiting to scale a rock face just a few hundred metres from Everest's summit when a snow ledge suddenly collapsed, flinging him off a ledge and shattering his left leg. As he lay on the slope in terrible pain, Harrod knew that being immobilised in Everest's 'Death Zone' (above 8000 metres) is usually a death sentence.

But his fellow climbers, Australian Peter Madew and American Walid Abuhaidar, who'd met Harrod just weeks before, were determined this wasn't going to be a usual case. The pair set about making a splint and used ropes to lower their friend down the mountain, metre by excruciating metre. Harrod needed more oxygen than usual due to the cold and pain, so his friends gave him what they had left of theirs. This meant Abuhaidar had to miss out on any last chance of returning to the summit and gaining the title he was so close to holding – youngest American via the North Ridge route.

When Harrod safely reached Sherpa help, seven long and exhausting hours later, both men said they could never have lived with themselves if they'd gone on to the summit instead of helping their new friend. By sticking by him, Abuhaidar and Madew had saved Harrod's life.

EXTREME SKIING

In 1970, Japanese adventurer Yuichiro Miura
(aged 37) carried skis and a parachute up to
South Col in an attempt to ski down Mount Everest.
When he gained speed he released the parachute,
but it barely slowed him because the air was so thin.
His skis couldn't dig in to slow him down because
the snow was so icy. He sped down 1830 metres in
two minutes! Just when he thought he was sure to
die, his ski caught a rock and he crash-landed into
soft snow, which saved his life. He became known as
'The Man Who Skied Down Everest'.

BE PREPARED

If you think that one day you may want to climb to the top of the world, here are some of the many things you'll need to do to prepare:

Decades before . . .

Start saving your money! Practise mountain craft, climbing, camping, hiking and survival skills on all sorts of mountains. Learn about Nepal and the people who live there.

Years before . . .

Get your body into the best shape of your life. Concentrate on your climbing skills and hike, with heavy packs, up and down steep hills at home. Go to Nepal and practise walking in crampons. Work on your rope, rescue and climbing skills on the biggest mountains in the world. Then practise some more!

PEAK CONDITION?

According to scientists, males reach their physical peak in their late twenties and females reach it in their mid thirties. Research also shows that plenty of exercise, good food, avoiding smoking and getting lots of sleep maintains peak performance at any age. A successful summit attempt also depends on determination, preparation and luck on the day. The youngest boy to summit Everest is Temba Tsheri, who was 15 years and 18 days when he did it in 2001. The youngest girl is Ming Kipa, a Sherpa who was 15 years and nine months old when she stood on the summit in May 2003. The oldest successful climber is Yuichiro Miura, the same Japanese adventurer who skied down Everest. He was 70 years and 222 days old when he stood on the summit on 22 May 2003.

Months before . . .

Work on acclimatising to the altitude and staying healthy. Eat well, sleep well and walk a *lot*. First walk to Base Camp, then up and down the mountain, each time gradually getting a little higher. Up down, up down . . .

Weeks before . . .

Continue your acclimatising hikes to the different high camps on the mountain: Camp 1, then Camps 2 and 3 . . . Be careful and listen to your guides and your own body. They'll help get you and your equipment in the best shape for the big challenge. If you are lucky, your body will let you go higher, and higher.

I THINK I'M GETTING THE HANG OF THIS!

The night before . . .

Camp at South Col – the world's highest campsite. Sleeping will be very difficult: you'll have trouble breathing, you'll feel too sick to eat, and it'll be extremely cold outside (perhaps minus 30 degrees Celsius). Not that you'll be in your sleeping bag long. You'll get up at 10 p.m!

At last, summit day . . . the final climb to the top of the world . . .

It might take two hours for you and your climbing partner to melt ice to drink and get ready. Remember, at altitude your brain is working *very* slowly, so something as simple as putting your socks on takes ages! By midnight you'll be ready to go. Just don't forget your oxygen mask, ice-axe and backpack!

You walk very slowly, single file, guided by the light of the very bright stars and your head torch. The windward side of your body is colder where the freezing wind hits, as is the hand carrying your metal ice-axe, because metal conducts the cold. To your left is the drop towards Base Camp. To your right, it's more than two kilometres straight down Kangshang Face to Tibet. In sections, there are safety lines to clip your harness into, but some don't look super-safe, so the best plan is – don't trip!

After many hours of step, pause, breathe, step, with cramponed feet, and bang, pause, breathe, bang, with your ice-axe, the sun rises. When you stop to swap oxygen cylinders, take a moment to peer through your goggles at the amazing view: fluffy clouds floating below you; white mountain peaks against an inky black sky; and in the distance – the curve of the Earth.

You pass landmarks on the route that show you're getting closer to your goal: a rocky outcrop called the Balcony, then South Summit, the Summit Ridge and the Hillary Step. Twelve hours since you left the tent: you're exhausted, but very close to the snowy summit of Mount Everest.

Step, pant, breathe, step. Bang, pant, breathe, bang . . . Finally a last thwack with your ice-axe, a last step up and – congratulations, you're on top of the world!

KIM WILSON's childhood involved being dragged on bush camps with khaki-clad boys by her Scout-leader mum. Despite the early horrors of finding squashed spiders deposited in her sleeping bag and mashed worms on her dinner plate, she went on to become an outdoor education teacher, keen world traveller and hiker, and editor of *Outdoor Australia* magazine, meeting many inspiring advernturers along the way.

ANDREW PLANT has illustrated over 120 books. He believes in thorough research and spent three weeks climbing to the Everest Base Camp ten years before this book was written! He got altitude sickness (and several disgusting stomach bugs) and was chased by an irate yak. He also proposed to his wife there – but she thought he said 'Will you carry me?'!

 Andrew is prepared to do even more research for a book on chocolates of the world.

THANKS

The author would like to thank:
- my patient and positive editing team: Eva Mills, Jodie Webster, Ruth Grüner (designer) and Sarah Brenan
- the super-talented illustrator, Andrew Plant
- fact-checking guru Lincoln Hall
- Jo Paul for kick-starting all this
- my own wonderful summit team of friends – especially Mum, Dad, Paul, Simi and TK, who've never stopped believing in me.

Kim Wilson

The publishers would like to thank the following for photographs used through the book:
- © Andrew Plant – page viii (Mount Everest), page 42 (Khumbu valley), page 54 (mountains around Khumbu glacier), page 76 (helicopter at Lukla), page 79 (bridge on trek to Base Camp), page 84 (Andrew with friend)
- © Sport the library/Roddy Mackenzie –page 21 (traversing crevasse), page 50 (tents in snow), page 64 (high altitude climbing)
- © Royal Geographic Society (www.rgs.org) – George Finch, page 28 (nude Mallory, 1922); Bentley Beetham, page 41 (ice formations, 1924); Charles Wylie, page 57 (boxes and preparations, 1953); Edmund Hillary, page 69 (Tenzing on summit, 1953); Alfred Gregory, page 71 (expedition team, 1953)
- istockphoto.com – Grafissimo (ice frame); Stefan Klein (photo frame); Georg Hafner, page 49 (crampon); Martin Kawalski, page 67 (woman trekking in Himalaya); Peter Hazlett, page 80 (climber)
- Peter Krohn, page 58 (Sherpa)

TIMELINE: FIRST OF THE FIRSTS

1953
First to summit (via South-east Ridge route)
Edmund Hillary & Tenzing Norgay

1960
First up the North-east Ridge route
Wang Fu-chou & Chu Yin-hua (China) & Konbu (Tibet)

1963
First up the West Ridge route
Tom Hornbein & Willi Unsoeld, USA

1975
First woman to summit
Junko Tabei, Japan

First up the South-west face
Doug Scott & Dougal Haston, UK

1978
First oxygen-free ascent
Reinhold Messner & Peter Habeler, Austria

1980
First solo ascent
Reinhold Messner, Austria

1984
First Australians to summit
Tim Macartney-Snape & Greg Mortimer

1988
First parachutist
Jean Marc Boivin (France) leapt off the summit with a parapente (a sort of parachute); eleven minutes later, he made a perfect landing on the Western Cwm

1990
First via North Ridge route
Tim McCartney-Snape, Australia

1995
First female oxygen-free ascent
Alison Hargreaves, UK

1997
First Australian woman to climb Everest
Brigitte Muir, Australia

1998
First amputee
Tom Whittaker, Wales (he'd lost his right foot in a car crash)

1999
Longest on summit
Sherpa Babu Chiri spent a record 21.5 hours on the summit

2001
First blind person to summit
Erik Weihenmayer, USA

WHERE TO FIND OUT MORE

Books

'Bushwalking and Mountaincraft Leadership,' (3rd ed.) Bushwalking & Mountaincraft Training Advisory Board, Victoria, 2000

Greg Child, *Mixed Emotions*, The Mountaineers Books, Seattle, 1997

George Craig, *Everest: 50 years of struggle to reach the top of the world*, Carlton Books, London, 2002

Paul Dowswell, *True Everest Adventure Stories*, Usborne, London, 2003

Edmund Hillary, *View from the Summit*, Corgi, London, 1999

Edmund Hillary, *High Adventure*, Allen & Unwin, Sydney, 2003

Jon Krakauer, *Into Thin Air*, Macmillan, New York, 1997

Richard Platt, *Everest: Reaching the World's Highest Peak*, Dorling Kindersley, London, 2000

Rebecca Stephens, *Everest*, Dorling Kindersley, London, 2001

Walt Unsworth, *Everest: the Mountaineering History*, The Mountaineers Books, Seattle, 2000

Stephen Venables, *Everest: Summit of Achievement*, Allen & Unwin, Sydney, 2003

Stephen Venables, *To the Top*, Walker Books, London, 2003

Websites

- www.mounteverest.net
- www.explorersweb.com
- imagingeverest.rgs.org
- www.nationalgeographic.com/everest
- www.pbs.org/wgbh/nova/everest
- www.panoramas.dk

HMMM – WONDER IF ITS TIME TO WASH THESE?

INDEX